21 Days of Faith and English

A Bible-Based Devotional for Students, Youth, and Families

Author: Marina Dunn

Let us remember our Creator
while we are young, grow in faith each day, and live an abundant life.
(Inspired by Ecclesiastes 12:1 and John 10:10, Holy Bible, King James Version.)

21 Days of Faith and English

A Bible-Based Devotional for Students and Adults

Author: Marina Dunn

For personal spiritual growth and learning.

Title: *21 Days of Faith and English*
Subtitle: *A Bible-Based Devotional for* Students, Youth, and Families
Author: Marina Dunn

First Edition: 2026
Printed in: India

ISBN (Paperback): 978-93-5717-175-5

eBook Edition available on Amazon Kindle

Publisher: Marina Dunn Publications

Dedication

This book is dedicated to every reader who desires to grow closer to God while growing stronger in English—students, teachers, parents, and all learners. May your faith grow deeper and your words become clearer.

A Note from the Author

As I prepared this devotional, I felt it was important to share why I chose **21 days**. Every number has meaning, and every day, season, and moment matters. The Bible reminds us that God knows us so deeply that even the hairs on our heads are numbered by Him.

In **Daniel 10**, we see how Daniel prayed and fasted, and after **21 days**, God's answer was revealed in a powerful way.

As I write this first book, I am also spending 21 days in prayer and fasting, asking God to renew my mind through His Word. This devotional is a space to meet God daily through His Word and be strengthened in His promises for you.

From around 2009 to 2017, I went through a time when I felt weak and too lost to return to God. Yet, in His mercy, Jesus revealed Himself to me. What I once felt as distance—the tears and the feeling that I could not return to Him—was actually **His Grace**, leading me to pray, seek forgiveness, and gently find my way back to Him. I am deeply grateful for His unfailing love, and I trust that He will continue to lead me **from Glory to Glory.**

Through personal experiences in my life and in the lives of my loved ones, I have seen God's promises proven true—His protection when hope seemed lost, and His miracles when things appeared impossible. This book invites you to journey through 21 days of faith, steadfast like Daniel, and to experience God increasing your faith as you are rooted in His Word. **God never fails.** He redeems time—He restores what seems lost and turns delays into purpose. Hold fast to His promises. What God has spoken, He will surely bring to pass.

With prayers,
Marina Dunn

Preface

This 21-day devotional is designed to strengthen your heart through God's Word while gently improving your English skills. Each day includes a Bible verse, a short reflection, an English Corner, a simple practice task, and a prayer. The language has been kept at a simple to intermediate level so that it can be easily understood by readers across various age groups.

May these pages help you build a daily habit of reading Scripture, reflecting, and speaking with confidence.

Thou wilt shew me the path of life: in thy presence is fullness of joy; at thy right hand there are pleasures for evermore.

— Psalm 16:11

How to Use This Book

1) Read the given verses slowly and carefully from your Bible.
2) Read the reflection and think about one lesson for your day.
3) Learn the words in the English Corner and use them in your own sentences.
4) Do the Practice activity (write and speak).
5) End with a short prayer—either the one given in this devotional or a prayer of your own, as the Holy Spirit leads you.

Tips:

Speak the "Speak it" line aloud twice to improve confidence and pronunciation.

Declare God's blessings and promises from His Word each day over your life and your loved ones.

DAY 1 — Known and Chosen

Verse: Jeremiah 1:5

Reflection: Before God formed you in your mother's womb, He knew you and set you apart for great works. Comparing yourself with others, sometimes makes you feel less important. But God sees value in you. He has a purpose for you. He calls you His own. When you feel unsure, remember: God knows your name and your future.

English Corner (Vocabulary):

• Purpose — a reason for something

• Formed — made or created

• Value — worth, importance

Practice: Write 1 sentence: "God has a **purpose** for my life."

Speak it: "I am chosen by God."

Prayer: Lord, thank You for You know me by my name. I am chosen by You. Help me walk in Your purpose. Amen.

DAY 2 — Loved and Saved

Verse: John 3:16–17

Reflection: God's love is not limited. Jesus, a gift from God, was given to us to save us. When we fail, God does not condemn us—He calls us to return to Him. Believe in His love for you which gives us hope, strength and a new start.

English Corner (Vocabulary):

- Condemn — declare guilty and punish
- Save — rescue
- Believe — trust in

Practice: Fill in the blank: God sent Jesus to ___ the world.

Speak it: "God's love gives me a new hope and a new beginning."

Prayer: Jesus, thank You for saving me. Help me believe deeply and live faithfully. Amen.

DAY 3 — Truly Free

Verse: John 8:36

Reflection: Freedom sounds like we can do **anything**. God's Word tells us that true freedom is freedom from sin, fear, guilt, and shame. Jesus breaks chains of anything that does not belong to His kingdom. When you belong to Christ, your older nature passes away and you become new —truly free.

English Corner (Vocabulary):

- Freedom — the state of being free
- Chains — things that bind or control
- Guilt — feeling bad for wrong actions

Practice: Write: "In Jesus, I am truly free."

Speak it: "Christ sets me free."

Prayer: Lord Jesus, thank You for freeing my heart. Teach me to live continually in Your freedom. Amen.

DAY 4 — Saved by Grace

Verse: Ephesians 2:8–10

Reflection: God has set us free. But how do we know this truth? God's Word in Ephesians 2:8–10 says that we are saved by grace through faith, not by our own efforts. God created us to live a life that shines His light. We need to learn and remember for the rest of our lives that we should not do good to be saved—we do good because we are saved.

English Corner (Vocabulary):

• Grace — God's undeserved kindness

• Effort — hard work

• Created — made

Practice:

Make 1 sentence using the word "grace."

Speak it: "I am saved by grace through faith."

Prayer: Father, thank You for Your grace. Help me to listen to Your Word daily so that I learn to have faith and to live a life full of good works. Amen.

DAY 5 — Crucified with Christ

Verse: Galatians 2:20; Galatians 5:24; 2 Corinthians 5:7,17

Reflection: When God's Word becomes our highest priority over our own desires, our new life begins. Sinful desires and wrong habits no longer control us. What's more, we start living by faith—believing that we are a new creation in Christ and finding our worth in Him. Our identity now dwells completely in Jesus Christ, our living Lord.

English Corner (Vocabulary):

- Faith — trusting God
- Identity — who you truly are
- New creation — a new life in Christ

Practice: Write: "I walk by faith, not by sight."

Speak it: "In Christ, I am new."

Prayer: Lord, help me live by faith each day and grow into the new person You made me to be. Amen.

DAY 6 — Strength in Weakness

Verse: 2 Corinthians 12:9

Reflection: We often hide our weakness, but God reminds us that His power is made perfect in weakness. When we admit our need for Jesus, His grace works in us more powerfully. As we walk with Him, we will see God reveal His power in the very areas where we once felt weakest.

English Corner (Vocabulary):

• Weakness — lack of strength

• Power — strength, ability

• Perfect — complete, best

Practice: Complete: "When I am weak, God is _____."

Speak it: "God's grace is sufficient for me."

Prayer: Lord, I give You my weaknesses. Strengthen me with Your grace. Amen.

DAY 7 — More Than Conquerors

Verse: Romans 8:26–39

Reflection: In our lowest moments, when words fail, the Holy Spirit intercedes for us and brings comfort, reminding us that God works all things together for good for those who love Him. God calls us more than a conqueror through Christ who loved us first. When you feel unworthy because of your mistakes, remember: nothing can separate you from His love. His Word is active, He can still work all things for your good.

English Corner (Vocabulary):

- Conqueror — winner, overcomer
- Separate — divide, remove
- Comfort — peace and support

Practice: Write: "Nothing can separate me from God's love."

Speak it: "God is for me, He is with me so I will prosper and prevail in doing good works for His greater glory."

Prayer: Father, thank You for Your never-failing love for me. Help me trust You in every situation. Amen.

DAY 8 — Greater is He

Verse: 1 John 4:4, 2 Timothy 1:7

Reflection: It is very common to be affected by the things happening around us and to fall into fear. But God says that He lives within us and He is greater than anything against us. He has given us His Spirit of power, love, and a sound mind, equipping us to live with courage. When fear rises, remember: God in you is greater.

English Corner (Vocabulary):

• Greater — bigger, stronger

• Fear — deep worry

• Courage — bravery

Practice: Write one fear you have. Then write: "God is greater than this."

Speak it: "Greater is He who is in me."

Prayer: Lord, help me face challenges with courage because You are in me, with me, and for me. Amen.

DAY 9 — Less of Me, More of Jesus

Verse: John 3:30

Reflection: Our fleshly desires push us to seek more for ourselves, but true growth begins when Jesus becomes first in our lives. As Christ increases, we become more humble, patient, and kind. Peace comes when we let Jesus lead and guide us.

English Corner (Vocabulary):

- Humble — not proud
- Increase — grow
- Lead — guide

Practice: Write: "Jesus, lead my life today."

Speak it: "Jesus must increase in me."

Prayer: Lord, remove pride from my heart. Help me live for You, not for myself. Amen.

DAY 10 — Life to the Full

Verse: John 10:10, Proverbs 6:31

Reflection: Jesus came to give us a meaningful life—an abundant life filled not only with comfort or wealth, but with peace, purpose, and joy. When John the Baptist said, "Jesus must increase, and I must decrease," he expressed the joy of surrendering to Christ, which leads to true abundance. The enemy seeks to steal and destroy, but Jesus, our Lord, is faithful to restore what is lost. A full life is simply a life that stays connected to Jesus each day.

English Corner (Vocabulary):

- Meaningful — full of purpose
- Destroy — ruin completely
- Restore — bring back

Practice: Write: "Jesus gives me purpose and peace."

Speak it: "In Jesus, I have abundant life."

Prayer: Jesus, fill my heart with Your joy and peace. Help me live fully in You. Amen.

DAY 11 — No Weapon Shall Prosper

Verse: Isaiah 54:17; Romans 8:31, Exodus 14:14. Revelation 5:5

Reflection: Troubles may come, but God's protection is stronger. "No weapon formed against you shall prosper" means attacks may happen, but they will not succeed. And if God is for us, no one can truly defeat us for Jesus has already won the battle, He has triumphed. Trust in God and the power of His might over your life for He is all-powerful.

English Corner (Vocabulary):

- Weapon — tool used to harm
- Prosper — succeed
- Protection — safety

Practice: Write: "God is for me, so I will not fear."

Speak it: "God protects me."

Prayer: Lord, protect me and my family. Help me stay fearless in Your promises. Amen.

DAY 12 — Walking in the Light

Verse: 1 John 1:7,9; John 8:12; John 1:5; Psalm 23:3; Philippians 4:8; Psalm 143:10, Psalm 37:23, Matthew 5:14-18

Reflection: Jesus is the Light of the world, and He calls us to walk in His light, to be His light and shine wherever we go. When we confess our sins, He is faithful to forgive and cleanse us, helping us focus our minds on what is good and live out His purpose for our lives—to shine His light. Remember: His grace is sufficient. He has made us His righteous sons and daughters; He restores our souls, guides our steps, and strengthens us through His Word.

English Corner (Vocabulary):

- Confess — admit honestly
- Forgive — remove guilt
- Focus — concentrate

Practice: Write three things that are true, noble, and pure. (Philippians 4:8).

Speak it: "Jesus is my light."

Prayer: Lord, keep me in Your light. Clean my heart, guide my thoughts and help me shine Your light. Amen.

DAY 13 — Guided and Rebuilt

Verse: Psalm 119:105; Isaiah 58:11–12, Isaiah 61: 3-4

Reflection: God's Word is a lamp for our steps. It is our map that gives us direction to the right path. God promises to guide us continually and to rebuild and restore every broken area. With Christ Who strengthens us, we can do all things, and with Him, nothing is impossible.

English Corner (Vocabulary):

- Guide — lead the way
- Rebuild — build again
- Direction — guidance

Practice: Write: "Your Word guides me daily."

Speak it: "God's Word is my lamp."

Prayer: Lord, guide me with Your Word and rebuild what is broken in my life. Amen.

DAY 14 — A Living Sacrifice

Verse: Romans 12:1–2

Reflection: God is pleased with a living sacrifice. A living sacrifice is when we offer our time, choices, problems, joys, sorrows and habits to God daily. We should not conform to the world's wrong patterns; instead, we must renew our minds through prayer and the Word. When our minds change according to the will of God, our lives are transformed for His glory.

English Corner (Vocabulary):

- Sacrifice — offering to God
- Renew — make new again
- Transformed — changed completely

Practice: Write one habit you want God to change in you.

Speak it: "Lord, renew my mind."

Prayer: God, transform my thinking and help me live a life that pleases You. Amen.

DAY 15 — The Lord is Faithful

Verse: 2 Thessalonians 3:3, Isaiah 55:11

Reflection: People may change, but God never changes. He is faithful to strengthen, protect, and establish you. When you feel uncertain, remember: God is your shield. His faithfulness is not based on your feelings—it is based on His nature. What He says is a promise we must claim over our lives, for the One Who spoke it, is faithful to fulfill it for our good and His glory.

English Corner (Vocabulary):

• Faithful — always trustworthy

• Strengthen — make stronger

• Protect — keep safe

Practice: Complete: "The Lord is faithful, and He will _____ me."

Speak it: "God is faithful to me."

Prayer: Lord, thank You for Your faithfulness. Strengthen and protect me today. Amen.

DAY 16 — Loved with an Everlasting Love

Verse: Jeremiah 31:3; Hebrews 13:8

Reflection: God's love is everlasting. It does not end when we fail. He promises never to leave us or forsake us. Jesus is the same yesterday, today, and forever. This means His love and power are steady. When everything around you changes, God remains the same.

English Corner (Vocabulary):

- Everlasting — never-ending
- Forsake — abandon
- Steady — firm, not changing

Practice: Write: "God loves me with an everlasting love and He will never leave me."

Speak it: "God, Your love for me never changes, for You are faithful to Your Word and You are the same yesterday, today and forever."

Prayer: Lord, thank You for being my God. Help me trust Your unchanging love. Amen.

DAY 17 — Not by Might

Verse: Zechariah 4:6; Philippians 4:13; Matthew 28:18; Ephesians 6:10

Reflection: Success is not only about talent or strength. God says victory comes by His Spirit. In Christ, you can do all things. Jesus has all authority, so we don't need to fear. Be strong in the Lord—not in yourself. When you depend on God, you rise higher.

English Corner (Vocabulary):

- Authority — power and right to rule
- Depend — rely on
- Victory — success, winning

Practice: Write: "I can do all things through Christ."

Speak it: "God's Spirit strengthens me."

Prayer: Holy Spirit, help me rely on You. Make me strong in the Lord. Amen.

DAY 18 — God Cannot Lie

Verse: Numbers 23:19; Genesis 18:14; Isaiah 43:13; Romans 8:31, Isaiah 55:11, Hebrews 11:1,3,6

Reflection: God always keeps His promises. He is not like humans who change their words. Nothing is too hard for Him. His Word will not return empty—it will accomplish what He wants. If God has spoken it, that settles it, it will happen. Trust His promises even if you cannot see results immediately. Remember, God is for you. Have faith in Him for God is pleased by your faith in Him.

English Corner (Vocabulary):

- Promise — a sure commitment
- Accomplish — complete successfully
- Immediately — at once

Practice: Write: "God's Word will come true."

Speak it: "Nothing is impossible for God."

Prayer: Lord, help me trust Your promises. Let Your Word work powerfully in my life. Amen.

DAY 19 — God Has a Plan

Verse: Isaiah 14:24,27; Jeremiah 29:11, Proverbs 3:5-6, Isaiah 55:11

Reflection: Trust God first —it's always a blessing. His plans for you are greater and they cannot be stopped. He has thoughts of peace and hope for your future. Even if you face delays or disappointments, God is still working. When you feel lost, remember: your future is not in fear—it is in God's hands —and His promises for you will never return empty.

English Corner (Vocabulary):

- Plan — a future purpose
- Disappointment — sadness from unmet expectations
- Hope — confident expectation

Practice: Write: "God has good plans for me."

Speak it: "My future is safe with God."

Prayer: Father, guide my future. Help me trust Your plan and not lose hope. Amen.

DAY 20 — The Living Word

Verse: John 1:1,14; Hebrews 4:12–13; Matthew 5:17–19; John 20:22; 1 Peter 1:23,24,25; John 6:63

Reflection: Jesus is the Word made flesh. The Bible is living and powerful—it speaks to our hearts and changes us. God's Word reveals what is inside us and leads us into truth. Jesus gives His Spirit, and His words give life. When you read the Bible daily, your spirit becomes strong.

English Corner (Vocabulary):

- Strong — full of strength
- Reveal — show clearly
- Spirit — God's presence within us

Practice: Read one verse aloud slowly, trusting in God's promises for you in His Word which is quick and powerful.

Speak it: "God's Word gives me life."

Prayer: Lord, make Your Word alive in me. Teach me truth and fill me with Your Spirit. Amen.

DAY 21 — Shine as Light

Verse: Matthew 5:14–16; John 14:26; John 20:22; Hebrews 12:28

Reflection: I remind you today that Jesus calls you the light of the world. You are meant to shine through your words, actions, and character. The Holy Spirit teaches and reminds you of God's truth. Since we belong to God's unshakable kingdom, we should live with gratitude and courage. Let your life be a message that brings greater Glory to God.

English Corner (Vocabulary):

• Shine — glow, show light

• Character — the kind of person you are

• Gratitude — thankfulness

Practice: Write one good deed you will do this week.

Speak it: "I will shine for Jesus."

Prayer: Holy Spirit, help me shine with kindness and truth. Use my life to bless others, bringing greater Glory to God in Jesus' Name I pray. Amen.

Vocabulary Index

- Accomplish
- Authority
- Believe
- Chains
- Character
- Comfort
- Condemn
- Confess
- Conqueror
- Courage
- Created
- Depend
- Destroy
- Direction
- Disappointment
- Effort
- Everlasting
- Faith
- Faithful
- Fear
- Focus
- Forgive
- Formed
- Forsake
- Freedom
- Grace
- Greater
- Guide
- Guilt
- Gratitude
- Hope
- Humble
- Identity
- Immediately
- Increase
- Lead
- Meaningful
- New creation
- Perfect
- Plan
- Power
- Strong
- Promise
- Prosper
- Protect
- Protection
- Purpose
- Rebuild
- Renew
- Restore
- Reveal
- Sacrifice
- Save
- Separate
- Shine
- Spirit
- Steady
- Strengthen
- Transformed
- Value
- Victory
- Weapon
- Weakness

May these 21 days continue as a lifelong walk with God.

www.ingramcontent.com/pod-product-compliance
Lightning Source LLC
LaVergne TN
LVHW090542110826
845146LV00003B/1239

* 9 7 8 9 3 5 7 1 7 1 7 5 5 *